STORIES OF JESUS · BOOK 2

THE BOY JESUS

BY

BETTY SMITH

Illustrated by   CICELY STEED

LUTTERWORTH PRESS · GUILDFORD, SURREY

Fifth impression 1982

STORIES OF JESUS

A beautiful new series of picture books, in which the great story is retold very simply and faithfully. Betty Smith is an Australian who has done much distinguished work for Sunday Schools and Christian education. Cicely Steed is one of the foremost illustrators of children's books, and her pictures with their clear outlines and rich colour are seen at their best in this series.

1 BABY JESUS   3 STORIES JESUS TOLD

2 THE BOY JESUS   4 FRIENDS OF JESUS

5 PEOPLE JESUS LOVED

6 JESUS AND THE CHILDREN

7 JESUS THE HEALER

8 JESUS, KING OF KINGS

BETTY SMITH

ILLUSTRATED BY CICELY STEED

ISBN 0 7188 1668 4

Printed in Hong Kong by Colorcraft Ltd.

CONTENTS

THE FLIGHT INTO EGYPT

THE three Wise Men had a dream, telling them not to let King Herod know where they found the Baby whose star they followed; telling them to return to their own lands by another way.

So, without seeing Baby Jesus again, the Wise Men left for their distant homes.

That same night, Joseph too, had a dream. He thought an angel stood beside him and said,

"Joseph! You must leave Bethlehem tonight. Baby Jesus is in danger. King Herod will try to kill Him. Go down to the land of Egypt."

When he awoke, Joseph was very anxious. He lit the lamp and, waking Mary, told her of his dream.

"We must leave at once," he said.

"While it is still night-time?" Mary asked.

"Yes, that is *why* we are going now. The darkness will hide us. No one must know which way

we take. You collect our things and get Baby ready. I'll saddle Joel."

As Mary packed the lovely gifts of the Wise Men, Joseph said,

"The lamb the shepherds gave must come too. He is used to being carried and will be no trouble."

Mary lifted little Jesus and held Him closely. How precious He was! Nothing must happen to her Baby. She wrapped Him snugly in a warm cloak. Then she whispered a prayer to God to take care of them all through their long journey.

Joseph was ready. He took Baby whilst Mary mounted the donkey, then handed Him to her. He laid down some money to pay for their lodging.

Taking the lamb on one arm, he caught the

donkey's bridle with his other hand. After a last look around, he blew out the lamp.

Out into the street he led Joel. *Clip*-a-clop, *clip*-a-clop went the uneven hoof-beats on the road. No one stirred or saw the little family, as their escape to Egypt began.

It was a worrying time. Mary could not help looking back every now and again. She held Baby Jesus very tightly. When she saw anyone coming,

she covered Him with her cloak. She had reason to fear. For wicked King Herod heard that the Wise Men had left for their own countries without seeing him again. He knew they must have found the Baby King in Bethlehem. He was so angry and jealous that he sent soldiers to kill every one of the baby boys in the town. But God's Son was far away in His mother's arms.

At last Mary and Joseph crossed the border into Egypt. Now they could relax and look about them. Everything was so very different from their own land.

Joseph did not wish to stay in the first cities they saw, so they went further south. They passed by the mighty Pyramids, very, very old even then. They did not know what lay ahead, but they were happy. For now Baby Jesus was quite safe.

"And the wise men, being warned of God in a dream, departed into their own country another way. And the angel of the Lord appeareth to Joseph in a dream saying, 'Arise and take the young child and his mother and flee into Egypt: for Herod will seek to destroy him.'"   Matt. 2: 12—13

THE HOME IN NAZARETH

THE baby days of Little Lord Jesus were spent beside the River Nile. This was the country that Joseph and Moses had known so many hundreds of years before. In an Egyptian city, a number of Jewish families had settled. Mary and Joseph joined them. There was always a demand for a good carpenter like Joseph, for the Egyptians made many lovely things of wood.

Months passed and Baby Jesus became Little Boy Jesus. He could run about and play in the warm sunshine. When He was two years old, some travellers from the north visited the Jewish settlers.

"Have you heard the news?" they asked. "King Herod is dead."

Mary and Joseph looked at each other. They had been happy in Egypt, but they longed for home. That very night, God spoke again to Joseph, "It is safe for you to return to your own land. Those who wished to kill the Child are dead."

Little Jesus was too small to understand why they were leaving Egypt, but He felt very excited.

He had to say "good-bye" for a while to his lamb, the shepherds' gift. It had grown too big to carry; but some friends of Joseph promised to bring it north with their own flocks shortly.

Soon they were on their way. Joel, the donkey, was now too old for Mary to ride. But they would not leave him behind. So he carried some of their things and trotted along near the other donkey. Sometimes Little Jesus walked beside Joseph, holding his hand. Sometimes He rode in front of His mother. Sometimes Joseph carried Him on his strong shoulders. The days flew by.

When Joseph reached Judea, he heard that Herod's son was now king. He would not risk staying there, but went further north still — back to Nazareth. How pleased Mary and Joseph felt to be in their own town once again! How proudly they showed Little Jesus to their friends and relations!

Nazareth lay in the hills of Galilee. Beyond the ridge ran the great Roman road, linking East to West. As Jesus grew older, He and other boys often lay in the grass, watching people pass along the road. Jesus loved to play, but sometimes He liked to be alone. Then, standing on a hilltop, He looked out across the valley to the distant mountains.

"This is My Father's world," He thought. "How lovely it is."

Stories of the great men of His race were told to Him — Abraham, Jacob, Joseph, Moses, Joshua, David, Solomon, Isaiah. Long afterwards, He could quote their words.

There was no school, but the eldest man in the village gathered the boys around him. There they learnt God's laws. For everything the Jewish people did was bound up in their religion.

At home, He helped Mary and Joseph. He rolled their sleeping mats tidily each morning. He filled the house lamps with oil. He made sure the tall jar was full of water to wash dust from the feet of guests. He fed the hens and animals and looked after them. They all loved their little Master, who only touched them with kindness.

Mary and Joseph taught Him everything Jewish boys must know. As His mother spun wool for their clothes, He sat beside her. He repeated after her the words of one of the first Psalms He learnt, Psalm 31. He never forgot the words, "Into thine hand I commit my spirit."

In springtime, Jesus saw farmers sowing their grain. He noticed some was taken by birds or choked by weeds. He saw that some fell into good soil; soon, green shoots appeared.

Out on the hills, shepherds looked after their sheep. At night, Boy Jesus often heard the men counting the sheep into the fold to make sure none was missing.

Sometimes there was a wedding in Nazareth, always at night. Jesus saw the bridesmaids going out to meet the groom. Their lamps shone like little fire-flies. Next day, the children played at weddings in the market-place.

Often there was sickness and sadness too, and Jesus longed to help. People said those in trouble were being punished for wrong-doing. Jesus felt this could not be right.

"My Father God *loves* everyone," He said to Himself. "When I'm grown-up, I'll do all I can to help those who are sick and poor."

In His own home, there was always love and kindness. Mary and Joseph trained the Boy given to their care to put God first, others second and Himself last.

"And they were in Egypt until the death of Herod. But when Herod was dead, an angel appeared to Joseph, saying, 'Take the young child and his mother and go into the land of Israel.' And he came into the land of Israel and turned aside into Galilee and dwelt in Nazareth." Matt. 2: 15—23

IN THE CARPENTER'S SHOP

EVERY Jewish boy learnt a trade. Nearly always, this was the same as his father's. As Joseph was a carpenter, he taught Jesus all he knew.

From the time He was tiny, Jesus spent part of every day in the workshop. The little Boy loved to play in the deep shavings of cedar and pine covering the floor. They had such a fresh, spicy smell. Often Mary brought her sewing and sat there to be near the two she loved. Husband and wife talked over the news. They spoke of the world outside — the world ruled by Rome. Sometimes they thought of the wonderful things that had happened on the night Jesus was born. They wondered what they all meant.

A village carpenter made many things. Stools, tables, and other furniture. Wooden ploughs and yokes for the necks of the oxen which drew them. Frames for doors and the doors themselves. Joseph passed on to Jesus all that he himself had learnt.

"A yoke is not easy to make," he said. "It must fit well. Don't make it so loose that it moves backwards and forwards. On the other hand, it must not grip tightly either. Run your hand down this one I'm making now."

"It's very soft and smooth," Jesus said, as His fingers passed over it.

"Yes, that's what I mean. If any hard, rough places are left, the animal will be sore. I've always made sure that my yokes are easy to wear."

Another day, Joseph was making a table. When Jesus handed him a board, he shook his head.

"No, my son. Not that one."

"Why not?" asked Jesus.

"You see that knothole and the crack running from it? It is not good timber. I know it would be underneath the table and no one would see it; but work that no one sees must be as good as the part seen by all. That is the way God wants us to build."

In the workshop, Jesus heard the men who came to give orders or collect finished goods. As they waited, they talked to Joseph and each other. Always it seemed to Jesus they said the same thing in different ways.

"If only we could free ourselves from Rome!"

"Look at the heavy taxes we must pay!"

"We are God's people. Has He forgotten us?"

"When the Messiah comes — God's Chosen One — then we shall be free."

"Yes, He will destroy the Romans. We shall have our own King again."

"It must be soon. All our prophets tell of His coming."

So it went on. The people of that land were very unhappy. Boy Jesus wished they would not be so angry. They were not even kind to each other.

The years passed quickly. At last Jesus was twelve years old. For the first time, Jesus was going with Mary and Joseph to the capital, Jerusalem. They were to attend the annual Feast of the Passover. This helped people remember that God had saved them from the Egyptians in the days of Moses.

A small group set out from Nazareth. Joined by others along the way, there was quite a crowd on the last day of the journey. What a wonderful moment it was, when they turned a corner of the road; there in the distance was the Temple —

God's House. Gleaming with gold, the white buildings shone in the sunlight. The people broke into a psalm of joy, and Jesus sang too —

"I was glad when they said unto me — let us go into the house of the Lord."

"And they returned into Galilee, to their own city, Nazareth. And the child grew, and waxed strong in spirit, filled with wisdom: and the grace of God was upon him." Luke 2: 39—40

JESUS IN THE TEMPLE

FOR a whole week, the city was crowded. It was a happy time for everyone. Old friends met again. There were many services to attend in the Temple. The best moment was the Passover meal. Then, dressed in outdoor clothes, they ate lamb, bread made without yeast, bitter herbs and other things. Each had a special meaning to remind them of God's help in the past.

The family from Nazareth was not always together. Mary visited her friends. Joseph talked with men he knew. Jesus was sometimes with them and sometimes with the other boys. More and more often, He went by Himself to the Temple. In a certain corner, the wise teachers, called Rabbis, sat. They answered questions people asked about God and His laws. Hour after hour, Jesus was there; He listened to all that was said.

All too soon, it was time to start for home. There

was a great bustle as the folk from the north set off. Mary could not see Jesus anywhere, but then she could not see Joseph either. Men and women usually travelled in two groups.

"They must be together," she said to a friend. "They'll come along later."

Towards evening, the men thought it was time to make camp. Presently Mary saw Joseph. He was alone.

"Where's Jesus?" she asked.

Joseph stared.

"Isn't He with you? I haven't seen Him all day."

"No — I thought He was with *you*. What can have happened to Him?"

"Now, don't worry," said her friend. "Perhaps He's talking to one of the other boys."

As the families camped for the night, the news spread.

"Has anyone seen the Boy Jesus today?"

No one had.

Mary and Joseph spent a dreadful night.

"If only I'd made sure He was with you," said Mary. "Where can He be?"

The moment it was light enough to see, Joseph saddled the donkey. Saying goodbye to their friends, husband and wife made their way back. With sad hearts, they saw again the busy city and shining Temple. From one friend to another they went.

"Has Jesus been here?" they asked, but no one had seen Him.

Three days dragged by. The two were almost

frantic. Where could their Boy be? What could have happened? At last, they went into the big Temple. Suddenly, Mary heard a boy's clear voice, asking a question.

She caught Joseph's arm.

"I heard His voice."

She looked all around, then pointed,

"There He is."

In front of the Rabbis sat Jesus. Mary hurried across.

"Jesus — oh, my son!" she cried. "How could you treat us like this? We have been beside ourselves with worry. We did not know where to look for you."

Boy Jesus turned. His thoughts had been far away.

"How was it you looked for Me? Didn't you know that I would be in My Father's house?"

Mary and Joseph didn't quite know what Jesus meant. They listened as the teachers praised the Boy. They heard of the wise questions He had asked. The Rabbis were very surprised at how much Jesus knew.

It was one more thing for Mary to remember,
after they went back to Nazareth. At home, Jesus
was always their true and loving Boy. Still, there
was a change in Him. For He had heard God's call
to His special work.

Many years would pass before He began teach-
ing and helping people, but from this time on-
wards, He thought about it always.

In that quiet little town, as Jesus grew older, He also grew closer to God.

"When he was 12 years old, they went up to Jerusalem. As they returned, Jesus tarried in Jerusalem: and Joseph and his mother knew not of it. And when they found him not, they turned back to Jerusalem. After three days, they found him in the temple. And his mother said, 'Son, why hast thou dealt thus with us?' And he said, 'Wist ye not that I must be about my Father's business?' And he went down with them to Nazareth and was subject unto them." Luke 2: 42—52